Animal discovery

Answers on pages 31 & 32!

Hey, Kids!

Each WORD FIND contains unlisted bonus words! Can you find them all?

The Animal Kingdom

The animal kingdom is made of up five main groups: mammals; birds; fish and sea animals; reptiles and amphibians; and insects and spiders.

Match a description of each group **to the right animal.**

Mammals have hair or fur.

Birds lay eggs.

Reptiles have scales.

Fish breathe underwater.

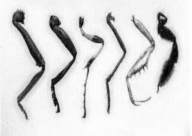

Insects have six legs.

iguana

carp

pelican

grasshopper

gorilla

Mammals

Mammals are a group of animals that have many things in common.
Most mammals live on land, some live in water, but none can breathe underwater.
Mammals have fur or hair (sometimes very little), and they feed their babies milk.

Can you think of some mammals?

_____   _____   _____

_____   _____   _____

Color the mammals!

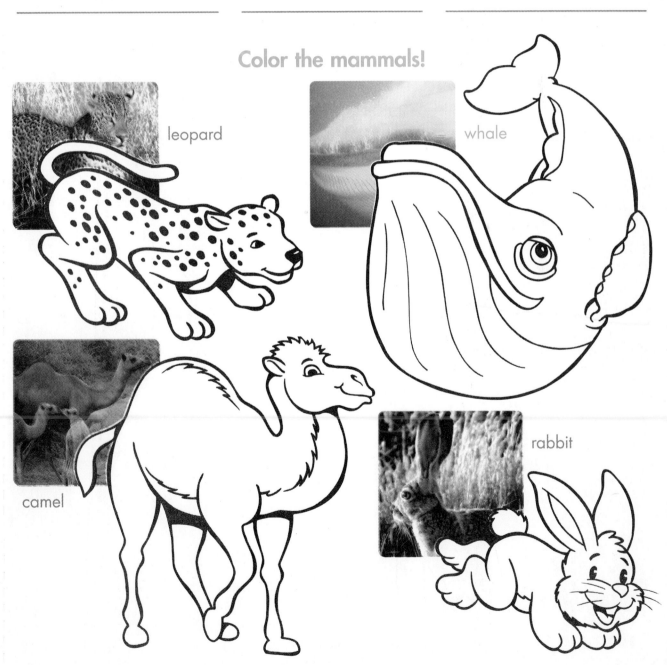

leopard

whale

camel

rabbit

Bat Find the difference between these two bat drawings.

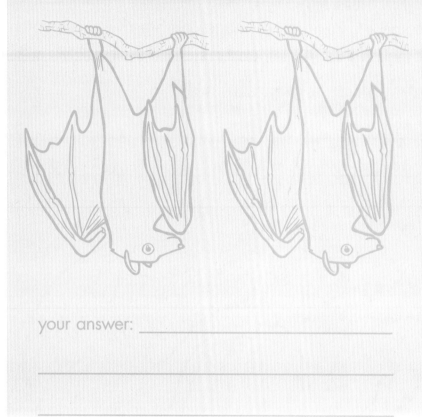

your answer: _____

_____

FUN FACT: Bats can catch insects in the dark! They find them by making clicking noises, then listening for the echoes that bounce off the insects.

Blue Whale Crack the code to fill in the rest of this sentence:

FUN FACT: The blue whale's heart is the size of a small car!

The blue whale is the

____ ____ ____ ____ ____ ____ ____

animal in the world.

🐇 = U   🐑 = L

🦭 = S   🦤 = D

🐊 = O

🐢 = T

🐘 = E

Camel

Unscramble the letters to find out the camel's nickname.

PISH FO

_____ _____

ETH TREDES

_____ _____ _____

FUN FACT: A camel can go for as long as two weeks without eating because it can live off the fat stored in its hump.

Chimpanzee

Which is the correct shadow of this chimpanzee?

 A

B

 C

your answer

FUN FACT: Chimpanzees are one of the only animals to use tools. They use rocks like hammers to break open nuts. They use plant stems like skewers to dig out termites.

Dolphin Use the grid to draw a dolphin.

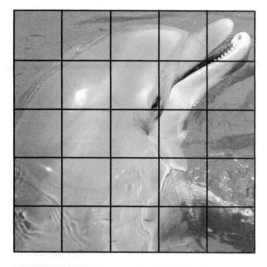

FUN FACT: Dolphins are marine mammals. They live together in groups and talk to each other using squeals or whistles.

Elephant Word Search: AFRICAN ASIAN BULL CALF COW TRUNK TUSK

African

Asian

K B M E M O R Y E A

N R U S C O W G W S

U O O L A T U S K I

R W R W L H E R D A

T N K A F R I C A N

FUN FACT: Elephants use their trunks for many things like eating, drinking, washing, feeling the ground for vibrations, and even to greet other elephants—like a handshake!

Giraffe Lead the giraffe across the savanna to the tall trees.

start

finish

FUN FACT: The giraffe is the tallest animal in the world, often stretching as high as a two-story house!

Hippopotamus

How many words can you make from the letters in:

HIPPOPOTAMUS

_____ _____

_____ _____

_____ _____

_____ _____

FUN FACT: A hippo is so heavy, it can walk along the bottom of a lake without floating up!

Kangaroo

Use the word bank clues to complete the crossword puzzle.

Kangaroos belong to a group of mammals called **marsupials**. Marsupial babies are born very small. They finish growing inside a pouch on their mother.

WORD BANK:
BOUND
TAILS
BABY
TUMMY
AUSTRALIA

ACROSS

1. A kangaroo _____ is called a joey.
2. The country where kangaroos live

DOWN

1. How kangaroos move; means the same as jump
3. A kangaroo baby tucks inside a pouch on its mommy's _____.
4. Kangaroos have long _____ that help them keep their balance.

FUN FACT: Kangaroos can't walk! They jump everywhere.

Koala Use the grid to draw a koala.

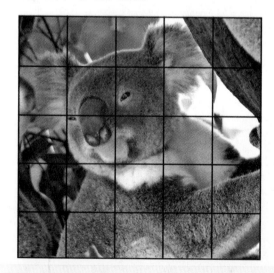

FUN FACTS: Koalas are marsupials that live in Australia, just like kangaroos. Koalas eat only one food—**eucalyptus leaves**—and they rarely drink.

Lion Unscramble the letters to find out the lion's nickname.

GINK FO

_ _ _ _   _ _

BASSET

_ _ _ _ _ _

FUN FACT: Female lions do most of the hunting for their family, or **pride.**

Panda

Which panda is different?

your answer

FUN FACT: A giant panda can eat up to 85 pounds of bamboo in a day!

Tiger Which is the correct shadow of this tiger?

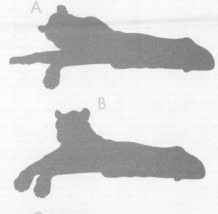

A

B

D

C

your answer

FUN FACT: The stripes on a tiger help it to hide better in tall grass.

Zebra

Which piece completes the picture?

FUN FACT: The stripes on a zebra serve as its defense. When a herd of zebras is grazing together, it is difficult for a predator to single out one zebra to attack.

A

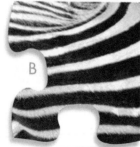
B

C

your answer

Birds

Most birds have feathers and can fly. Birds have good
hearing so they can answer the songs of other birds.
Birds lay eggs, and many build nests to keep them safe and warm.

Color the birds!

toucan

vulture

chicken

kiwi

Eagle

Use the word bank clues to complete the crossword puzzle.

WORD BANK:
TALONS
EYESIGHT
UNITED STATES
BALD
EAGLET

ACROSS

2. An eagle is sometimes said to look _____ because of the white feathers on its head.
4. The bald eagle is the national bird of the _____ _____.

DOWN

1. A baby eagle is called an _____.
3. Eagles are known for their amazing _____ because they can see small prey from far above.
5. Eagles have sharp, black _____ on their feet.

FUN FACT: Eagle nests can be as big as 8 feet across!

Flamingo

Because of the shape of its beak, a flamingo must eat with its head

Crack the code to figure out the rest of the sentence.

🐗=W   🐘=E   🦏=U   🐈=D
🐃=N   🐧=P   🦌=I   🐿=O   🦑=S

FUN FACT: Some flamingo colonies have as many as 10,000 birds!

Hummingbird Help the hummingbird migrate south.

start

finish

FUN FACT:
Hummingbirds beat their wings in a figure-eight pattern. Some species flap 80 times a second!

Ostrich Word Search:

FLIGHTLESS FLOCK LARGEST
RUNNING GRASSLAND EYELASHES

FUN FACT: Ostriches are the fastest bird runners in the world, reaching speeds of 45 miles per hour. That's faster than a racehorse!

```
D A C V T Z B L A C K F E A T H E R S G H
E Q S R W A E X Y C M F G R A S S L A N D
S F D G U H L Z O L D B G C U Z N A O Z P
E T S E G R A L K G O P S Q I N V W T D K
R E S I E A F L I G H T L E S S N L A F J
T B C F J V M T M N P L U M E S R I D M O
H E Y E L A S H E S C L P D K T J Q N P E
I B D T U Q W Y S R E H T A E F Y A R G B
```

Owl Which piece completes the picture?

FUN FACT: Owls' eyes never move. To look around, an owl relies on its very flexible head and neck. Owls can sit up straight and turn their heads upside down!

your answer

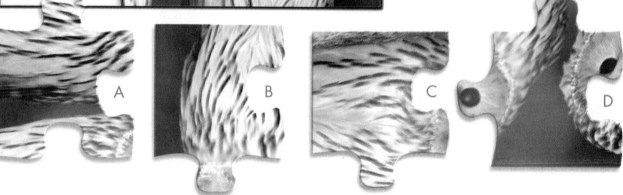

A   B   C   D

Parrot Find and circle the difference between these two parrots.

FUN FACT: Parrots are often loud and noisy, and they can sometimes mimic human speech.

Peacock Which is the exact mirror image of this peacock?

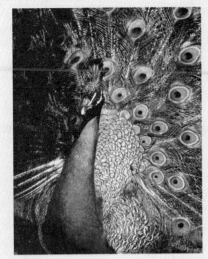

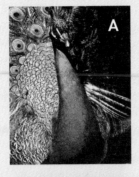
A

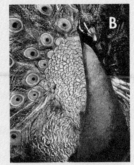
B

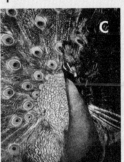
C

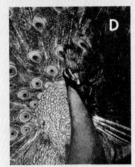
D

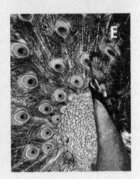
E

your answer

FUN FACT: A peacock's long tail feathers are called his train. Some trains can reach 8 feet high and 5 feet wide!

Penguin Use the grid to draw a penguin.

FUN FACT: Penguins cannot fly and they find it hard to walk. They often move by sliding on their bellies over the ice!

Turkey Unscramble the letters to find out which country almost made the turkey its national bird.

TUNEDI SETTAS

_____   _____

FUN FACT: A male turkey is called a *tom*. A female is called a *hen*.

Woodpecker How many words can you make from the letters in:

WOODPECKER

_____   _____

_____   _____

_____   _____

_____   _____

_____   _____

_____   _____

FUN FACT: Woodpeckers chisel into wood to make nests and to find insects and sap to eat.

Fish and Sea Animals

Fish have been around for **400 million years**! They can breathe underwater with their gills. There are over 24,000 types of fish.

Color the sea creatures!

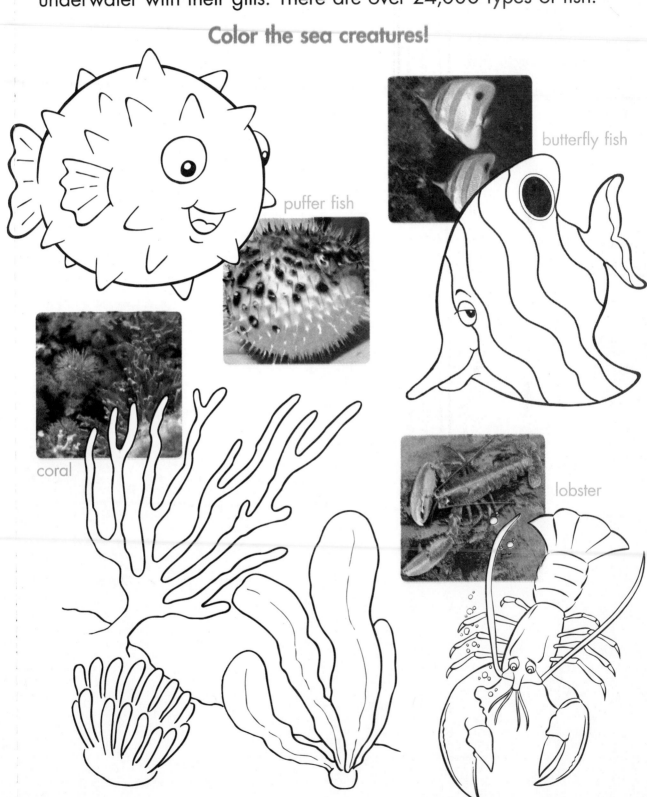

butterfly fish

puffer fish

coral

lobster

Crab Help the crab cross the maze so it can lay eggs on the beach.

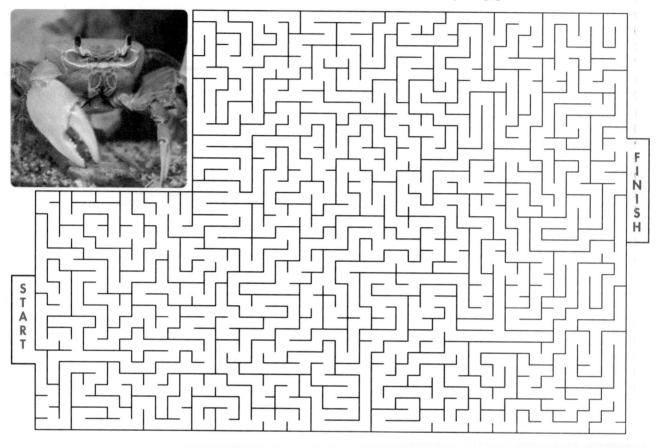

FUN FACT: Some crabs are as big as car tires!

Octopus Word Search:

EIGHT PROPEL SUCKERS TENTACLES
MOLLUSK TOOTHLESS INK (8 TIMES!)

FUN FACT: Some octopuses can change the color of their body—and they can squirt an inky substance!

B	P	T	L	S	U	E	M	C	W	C	D	S	I	V	K	L	T	M	N	D	M
A	R	M	S	F	K	S	U	L	L	O	M	N	T	E	N	T	A	C	L	E	S
K	O	N	Y	N	N	O	L	L	U	S	K	G	H	S	I	F	L	I	V	E	D
N	P	H	I	O	I	D	P	K	N	I	Q	R	B	S	Z	N	A	R	O	P	K
I	E	I	G	H	T	O	O	T	H	L	E	S	S	U	C	P	K	R	S	N	Z
V	L	J	W	I	V	O	J	S	R	E	K	C	U	S	A	O	D	B	I	Y	C

Ray

Crack the code to figure out the missing word in this sentence.

FUN FACT: Manta rays are the largest rays. They can grow to be 20 feet across. *That's wider than a car is long!*

Some rays have

_ _ _ _ _ _

on their tails that can sting a predator.

🦌 = I   🐧 = P   🐚 = S   🐘 = E   🦃 = N

Sea Horse

How many words can you make from the letters in:

SEA HORSE

FUN FACT: A mother sea horse lays her eggs inside a pouch on the *father's* tummy. The father actually *gives birth* to the babies!

Shark

Use the word bank clues to complete the crossword puzzle.

ACROSS

3. This type of shark looks like it could pound nails.
5. When a shark hunts, sometimes its _____ pokes out of the water.

DOWN

1. Some sharks are born in a tiny egg case, called a _____.
2. Sharks' skeletons are made of _____.
4. Sharkskin is so _____, it was once used as sandpaper.

FUN FACT:
A shark may lose 30,000 teeth in a lifetime.
A shark can grow a new set of teeth every two weeks!

Starfish

Which is an exact match of this starfish?

FUN FACT: A starfish has eyes on the end of each arm!

A   B   C

your answer

WORD BANK:

HAMMER-HEAD

PURSE

FIN

ROUGH

CARTILAGE

Reptiles and Amphibians

Reptiles and amphibians are cold-blooded, which means they are the same temperature as the air or water around them. They can live on land and in water, though they breathe air. Most lay eggs. Many smell with their tongues.

Color the reptiles and amphibians!

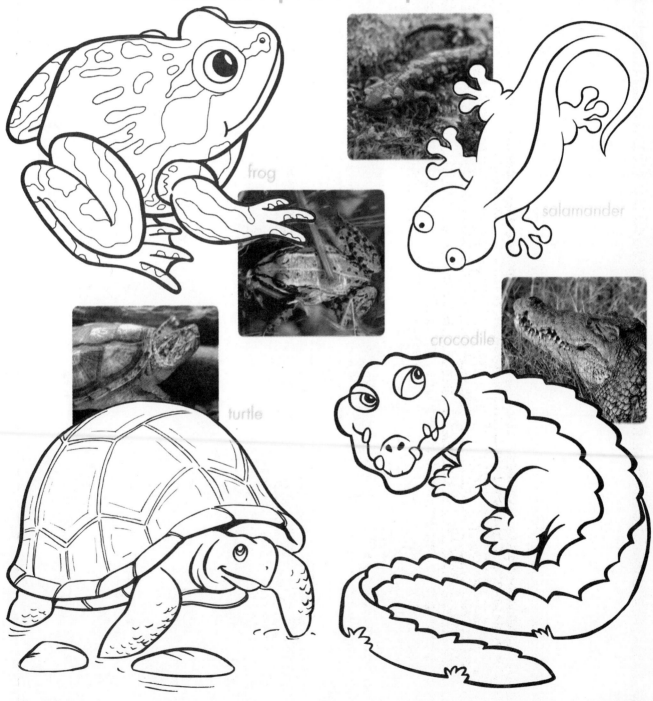

frog

salamander

turtle

crocodile

Alligator

Which piece completes the picture?

FUN FACT: Alligators and crocodiles are closely related. However, an alligator has a shorter, broader snout than a crocodile, and its teeth are hidden when its mouth is closed. They have lived on Earth for 65 million years!

your answer

A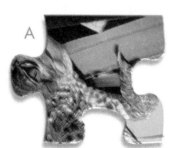

B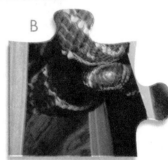

C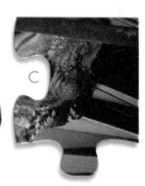

Chameleon

Circle the 3 differences between these chameleon pictures.

FUN FACT: Chameleons can change color to hide from enemies. They also change color when they are frightened or angry.

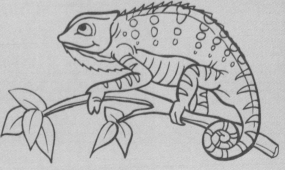

Cobra Crack the code to figure out the rest of this sentence.

A spitting cobra can squirt

_____ _____ _____ _____ _____ _____

at its victims.

🐊=O 🐰=N 🐦=I 🦐=S 🐧=P

FUN FACT: The cobra is well known for its hood, a flap of skin behind its head that it can flare when it feels threatened.

Rattlesnake

Word Search: RATTLE MOLT VENOM VIPER FANGS TAIL SWIMMER

```
D A K C R E H T I L S
I Q F A N G S D R E U
A E H H C T K I F S O
M I Q F D R I O P N N
O M E S G T N S R T O
N A L V W A T E A H S
D U F C O I L G T U I
B K I K R L M N T C O
A E V E N O M M L B P
C T P O Y B P O E J H
K I X Z L J Z L M R W
V B M Y K G L T P V Z
```

FUN FACT: A rattlesnake gets its name from the hollow scales on the tip of its tail. When a rattlesnake wants to send a warning to predators, it shakes its tail. The shaking sounds like a baby's rattle.

Tortoise Use the grid to draw a tortoise.

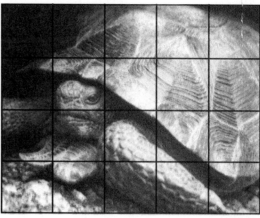

FUN FACT: The Galapagos tortoises can grow to be 6 feet long—**that's as long as a man is tall!**

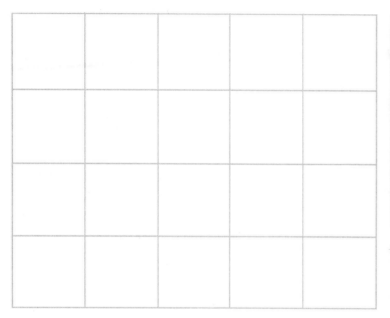

Toad Unscramble the letters to find out how the European common toad defends itself.

FUN FACT: Toads and frogs are closely related, but toads usually have bumpier skin. Also, toads often move by **crawling** rather than jumping.

SOBWL PU

_ _ _ _ _   _ _

KEIL A NOOBLLA

_ _ _ _   _   _ _ _ _ _ _ _ _.

Insects and Spiders

Insects have six legs; spiders have eight. Both are invertebrates, which means **without a backbone.** Many of these creatures can fly, and many have an exoskeleton, which means a skeleton on the outside of the body. There are more insects than any other type of animal in the world. Fossils prove that they've been on Earth since at least 150 million years before the dinosaurs!

Color the insects and spiders!

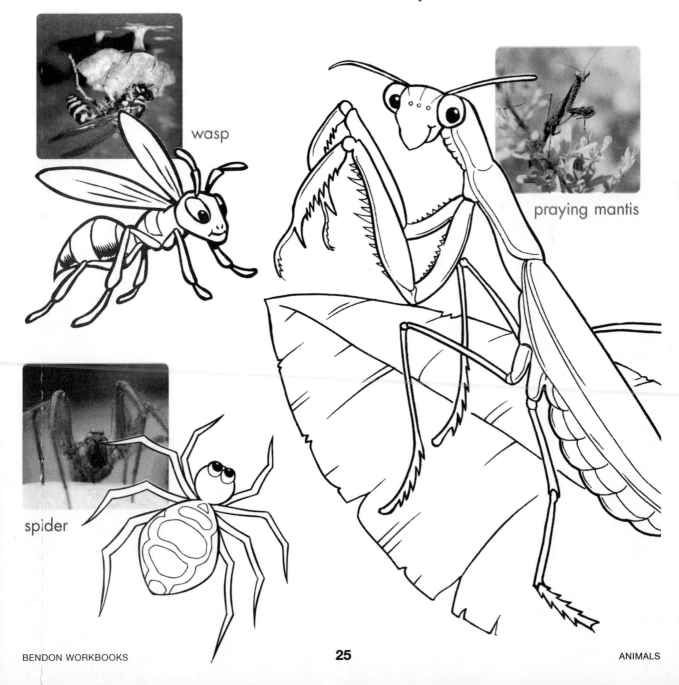

wasp

praying mantis

spider

Bee Use the word bank clues to complete the crossword puzzle.

ACROSS

2. There is one mother bee in every colony, called the _____ bee.
3. Bees collect pollen and turn it into _____. Yum!
5. Bees gather this yellow powder from flowers.
6. When bees are disturbed, they might _____. Ouch!

DOWN

1. Some bees _____ in circles to tell other bees where to find food.
3. Bees live in a colony in a _____.
4. Male bees are called _____.

FUN FACT: Bees have special baskets on their legs to collect pollen.

WORD BANK:
DRONES
HONEY
STING
QUEEN
DANCE
HIVE
POLLEN

Ant Help the leaf-cutter ant drag the leaf to the anthill.

start

finish

FUN FACT: There are about one quadrillion ants on Earth—that's **1,000,000,000,000,000!** There are more than 8,000 different kinds of ants. They live on almost all land areas.

Butterfly

Which butterfly is different? Color all the butterflies.

A

your answer

B

C

FUN FACT: Butterflies use their antennae for smelling. A butterfly keeps its tongue, called a **proboscis**, rolled up until it wants to eat. Then the butterfly unrolls it and uses it like a straw.

Caterpillar

FUN FACT: Swallowtail caterpillars have the ultimate camouflage—they look just like bird droppings. No animal would want to eat that!

How many words can you make from the letters in:

CATERPILLAR

Cricket

Which piece completes the picture?

FUN FACT: Crickets have wings, but most do not fly. They use a special "organ" on their wings to make their famous music!

your answer

A

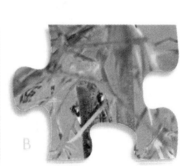

B

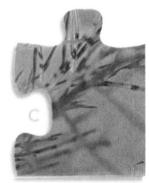

C

FUN FACT: Dragonflies are among the oldest living creatures. They've been on Earth more than 300 million years!

Dragonfly

Crack the code to figure out the rest of this sentence.

Dragonflies are known as air

___ ___ ___ ___ ___ ___ ___ ___

because they can fly forward or backward; they can even hover!

 = T   = R   = O   = A   = B   = S   = C

Firefly

FUN FACT: Fireflies flash and wink their "tail lights" to talk to other fireflies.

Unscramble the letters to find out another name for baby fireflies or *larvae.*

ROMWGWLOS

_ _ _ _ _ _ _ _

FUN FACT: Ladybugs don't have ears. They use their feet to sense vibrations, which allows them to know when predators are near.

Ladybug

How many spots do you count on these ladybugs?

your answer

Spider Use the grid to draw a spider.

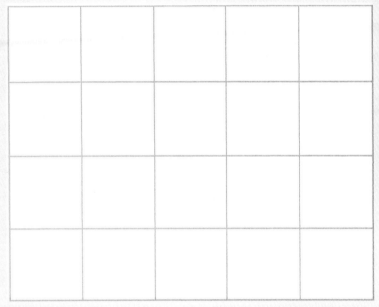

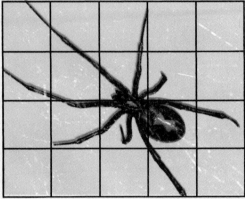

FUN FACT: A spider is an arachnid—not an insect. It has eight legs and two main body parts.

Tarantula Word Search:

WEB SPIN SILK ARACHNID FIGHT
TRAP POISON PREY TARANTULA

FUN FACT: A thread of spider silk is stronger than a steel thread of the same thickness. A one-inch-thick rope made of spider silk could pull 50 automobiles at once!

```
E W H I P O I S O N P P A R K E R G O F
T O W E B L T A W M S F Q R O P B Y X Z
I D J I A W P Y N I P R E Y A Z G Z A Y
B I H G I A M F L E I K G Z H C V M E S
L W D H R B Q K D K N L J B F L H F N Y
A S V T C E S B C E R N W O R B E N P U
C A Y R I A H F I D D L E B A C K G I M
K P R E D A T O R A L U T N A R A T S D
```

Answer Pages

Answer Pages

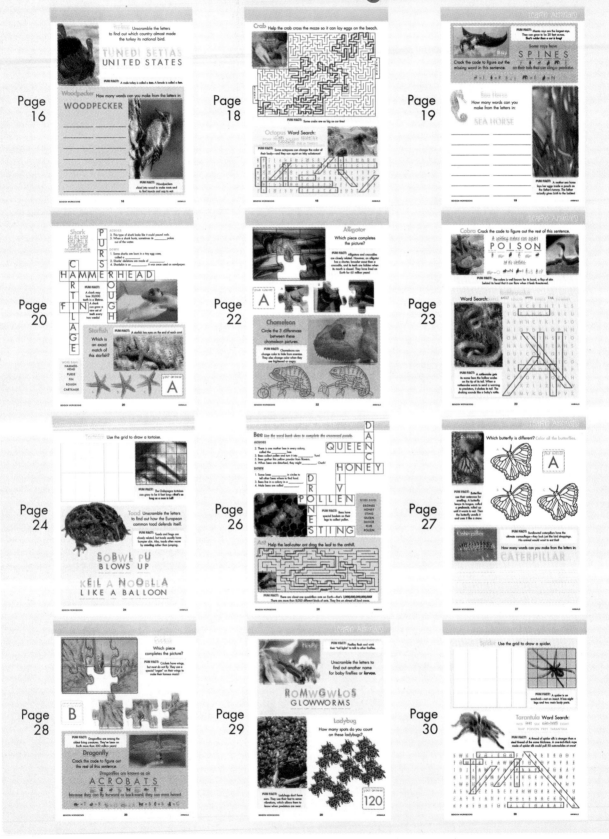

Page 16

Page 18

Page 19

Page 20

Page 22

Page 23

Page 24

Page 26

Page 27

Page 28

Page 29

Page 30